KT-439-520

Contents

Introduction

Gabriel watched every morning for the girl's visit to the fields. Her bright eyes, her long black hair and her quick laugh became more attractive to him every day. In fact, love – that quiet thief – was slowly beginning to steal young Farmer Oak's heart.

Gabriel Oak has worked hard all his life and knows what he wants. And when he meets Bathsheba Everdene, he is soon sure that he wants to marry her. But Bathsheba has other ideas – beautiful and independent, she is not ready to marry yet. When Gabriel loses his farm, he knows that he has lost all hope. But 'love is a golden prison,' so when Bathsheba asks for his help on her own farm, he cannot say 'no'. Even when she falls in love with the handsome but selfish Sergeant Troy, Gabriel refuses to leave her. Is he a fool, or her only true friend? And will Bathsheba's beauty bring her happiness, or life-long pain and sadness?

A story of hard lives and strong feelings, *Far from the Madding Crowd* is a book that few people can forget.

Thomas Hardy was born in 1840, in Upper Bockhampton, a small village near Dorchester in the south-west of England. His father was a builder and stonecutter. Thomas was educated at local schools and then got a job in a local builder's office, where he worked for ten years. In 1861 he moved to London and studied at evening classes. He began to write stories. One of his early books was *Under the Greenwood Tree* (1872), a gentle, humorous picture of love and marriage in a Dorset village. The book was quite successful and he decided to become a professional writer. In 1874, he married Emma Gifford, a musician, and completed *Far from the Madding Crowd*, which

Far from the Madding Crowd

THOMAS HARDY

Level 4

Retold by Jennifer Bassett
Series Editors: Andy Hopkins and Jocelyn Potter

Pearson Education Limited
Edinburgh Gate, Harlow,
Essex CM20 2JE, England
and Associated Companies throughout the world.

ISBN 0 582 41764 3

Far From the Madding Crowd was first published in 1874
This adaptation first published by Penguin Books 1991
Published by Addison Wesley Longman Limited and Penguin Books Ltd. 1998
New edition first published 1999

3 5 7 9 10 8 6 4 2

Designed by D W Design Partnership Ltd
Typeset by RefineCatch Limited, Bungay, Suffolk
Set in 11/14pt Monotype Bembo
Printed in China
SWTC/02

For a complete list of titles available in the Penguin Readers series, please write to your local
Pearson Education office or to: Penguin Readers Marketing Department,
Pearson Education, Edinburgh Gate, Harlow, Essex CM20 2JE.

appeared in the Cornhill Magazine. This story already has some of the sadness and seriousness that are to be found in Hardy's later work. Other stories followed: *The Mayor of Casterbridge* (1886), *The Woodlanders* (1887), *Tess of the D'Urbervilles* (1891) and *Jude the Obscure* (1896).

Hardy had a deep understanding of the poorer people in society and of the passions which people of any class feel. At the same time he was an admirer of Darwin's writings and realized that very often human beings cannot control their lives or change the course of events. Most of his stories end unhappily.

In 1883, Hardy went back to live in Dorset. In his later years he stopped writing stories and wrote poems, most of them produced after he was seventy. He believed that the language of his poems should be as close as possible to spoken language. His poems have great simplicity and some readers value them more highly than his stories. *Wessex Poems and Other Verses* came out in 1898 and was followed by other collections.

In 1910, Hardy was given the Order of Merit by the king, in recognition of his work. He married for the second time in 1914 and died in 1928 at the age of eighty-eight.

The girl held up the mirror to look at her face. Unseen in his field,
Gabriel Oak smiled to himself in amusement

Chapter 1   An Offer of Marriage

Farmer Oak was a strong, well-built man, with a wide smile that reached from ear to ear. His first name was Gabriel, and his comfortable old clothes and quiet way of walking about his fields showed him to be a calm, sensible man. He was hard-working, had intelligent opinions, and went to church on Sundays. His neighbours generally thought well of him.

He was at the best age for a man. The confused feelings and thoughts of a very young man were behind him, and he had not yet arrived at the time when he had to carry the heavy responsibilities of a wife and family. In short, he was twenty-eight and unmarried.

On a sunny morning in December, Oak was walking across one of his fields. Next to the field was a road, and Oak could see a wagon moving slowly along. The wagon was full of furniture and boxes, and on the top of all these things sat a woman, young and attractive. As Oak watched, the wagon came to a stop.

'One of the boxes has fallen off, Miss,' said the wagoner.

'Oh, then I think I heard it fall not long ago,' the girl said.

The wagoner ran back to find the box and for a few minutes the girl sat without moving. The only sounds were birds singing. Then she suddenly picked up a small paper packet, opened it, and took out a mirror. She quickly looked round to see if she was alone, then held the mirror up to look at her face. As she looked, her lips moved, and she smiled.

The sun shone down on the girl's bright face and dark hair, and the picture was certainly a pretty one. But it was an odd thing to do when travelling on an open wagon. The girl did not tidy her hair or do anything; she just looked at her own face. Still unseen in his field, Gabriel Oak smiled to himself in amusement.

1

When the wagoner came back, the girl put away her mirror and the wagon moved on down the road. Oak followed it slowly, and when he came near the gate at the bottom of the hill, he heard the girl arguing with the gatekeeper. She was refusing to pay the extra twopence that the gatekeeper asked for, and after a few minutes the girl won the argument. The gate was opened, and the wagon drove on. The gatekeeper watched it go.

'That's a handsome girl,' he said to Oak.

'And she knows it – too well,' said Gabriel, thinking of the mirror.

♦

In the next few weeks, Oak saw the girl again several times. She had come to live with her aunt in the village, and was often in the field next to Gabriel's, milking her aunt's cow. Once, Gabriel found her hat for her when it had blown off in the wind. She spoke a few words to him then, and after that meeting Gabriel found that the girl's lovely face was often in his mind.

It was the time of year when the sheep had their lambs, and Gabriel spent a lot of time in the fields, looking after his sheep and the new lambs. This was his first year as a farmer; before that he had worked on other people's farms, as a shepherd or a farm manager. He had worked hard and borrowed money to start his own farm with two hundred sheep, so it was an important time for him.

But although he was busy with his sheep, Gabriel watched every morning for the girl's visit to the fields. He learnt that her name was Bathsheba Everdene, and her bright eyes, her long black hair and her quick laugh became more attractive to him every day. In fact, love – that quiet thief – was slowly beginning to steal young Farmer Oak's heart. And one day he said to

2

himself, 'I'll make her my wife. I'll never be happy without her.'

So a few days later, he put on his best clothes, and went down to the village. When he got to the house, only the aunt was at home, but as he came away from the village, he met Bathsheba coming down the hill. They stopped, and looked at each other.

Farmer Oak had had no practice in asking girls to marry him, and he did not quite know how to begin.

'I've just been down to your house, Miss Everdene,' he said. 'I came to ask if you'd like to marry me.' He paused. 'But perhaps you've got a young man already.'

'Oh no!' The girl shook her head quickly. 'I haven't got a young man at all.'

Gabriel looked pleased. 'I'm truly glad to hear that,' he said, smiling one of his long, special smiles. He held out his hand to take hers, but she hurriedly put her hand behind her back.

'I'm not sure if I want to marry anyone,' she said, her face a little pink.

'Come,' said Gabriel quickly, 'think a minute or two. I love you dearly, Bathsheba, and I'm sure I can make you happy. I have a nice little farm, and when we are married, I'll work twice as hard as I do now. And in a year or two you can have a piano . . . And a nice little wagon to go to market.' He watched her hopefully.

'Yes, I would like that.'

'And you'd have chickens,' continued Gabriel, as the ideas came to him. 'And a little garden for flowers and vegetables.'

'I'd like that very much.'

'And at home by the fire, whenever you look up, there I shall be . . . And whenever I look up, there you will be.'

'Wait, wait! You're in too much of a hurry, Farmer Oak!' Bathsheba stared thoughtfully at a small tree. Then she turned to Gabriel.

'No, it's no good,' she said at last. 'I don't want to marry you. A wedding would be nice, it's true. But a husband . . . Well, he'd always be there, as you say. Whenever I looked up, there he would be.' She shook her head. 'No, I don't think I want a husband, so I won't marry – not yet.'

'That's a silly thing to say!' said Gabriel quickly. 'But my dear,' he continued sadly, 'why won't you have me?'

'Because I don't love you, Mr Oak.'

'But I love you,' said Mr Oak, very seriously. 'And one thing is certain. I shall go on loving you until the day I die.'

'I'm very sorry,' Bathsheba said. She looked sad for a moment, then she gave a little laugh. 'No, Mr Oak, I'm not the right wife for you. I'm too independent, and you wouldn't like that, you know.'

Oak heard the decision in her voice, and felt that his chances were finished. 'Very well,' he said quietly. 'Then I'll ask you no more.'

♦

When a man has begun to love, it is not easy to stop loving. Soon after, Gabriel heard that Bathsheba had left the village and gone to live at Weatherbury, twenty miles away. But this news did not put out the slow-burning flame of love in Gabriel's heart.

Chapter 2   A Fire in the Farmyard

Two months had passed, and Gabriel Oak was in the marketplace in the town of Casterbridge, looking for work as a shepherd. He was Farmer Oak no longer. One disastrous night a young dog had driven his sheep over the edge of a very steep hill, and most of the sheep and their lambs had fallen to their deaths below. Oak was just able to pay back the money he had borrowed to start his farm. After that, he was a free man with the clothes on his back, and nothing more.

Although he smiled less often now and his eyes were sadder, he was a man of quiet good sense and showed a calm face to the world. But that day in Casterbridge the world had no job to offer him, and at nightfall Oak set off on the road towards Weatherbury to visit another market the next day. The name of Weatherbury had some magic for him, since that was where Bathsheba Everdene now lived.

After a time, Oak stopped to rest, and as he sat on a gate, he saw a red light in the night sky across the fields. He watched, and the light grew brighter. Something was on fire. He jumped down from the gate and ran across the fields towards the fire.

When he arrived, he saw that the fire was in a farmyard. A tall pile of new-cut straw was burning wildly, flames shooting into the sky. It was too late to save that pile, but through the clouds of smoke Oak saw that there were several more straw-piles nearby. All the corn of the farm was there – and in great danger of burning. Already tongues of flame were beginning to reach out greedily towards the next pile.

Men were running here and there in the farmyard, but Oak saw that nobody was doing anything useful. He ran quickly towards the burning straw-pile and shouted to the men.

'Bring a ladder – quick! And buckets of water.'

'The ladder is burnt,' shouted one of the men.

Quickly, Oak climbed up the steep side of the next straw- pile. Coughing in the thick smoke, he sat dangerously on the top, and with his shepherd's stick he put out each finger of flame that came from the burning straw a few yards away. Soon buckets of water were passed up, and slowly Oak and the other men began to win the fight against the fire.

At one end of the farmyard, away from the smoke and confusion,
were two women, one of the women was on horseback.

At one end of the farmyard, away from the smoke and confusion around the fire, were two women, watching with worried faces. One of the women was on horseback, the other on foot.

'He's a shepherd, I think,' said the woman on foot. 'He's a fine young man, Miss!'

'I wonder whose shepherd he is,' said the woman on horseback. She called to a man who was passing. 'Jan Coggan! Who is the shepherd?'

'I don't know, Miss. He's a stranger,' replied Jan Coggan. 'But he's a brave man. He's saved your corn for you.'

'Yes. And I'm very grateful to him,' said the rider. 'Ask him to come and speak to me.'

The fire was beginning to die now, and Gabriel had climbed down. He thought of asking for a job here – he had learnt from one of the villagers that the farmer was a rich young woman. Her uncle had died recently and the farm was now hers.

Jan Coggan led Gabriel over to the woman on horseback. Gabriel's clothes were burnt into holes, and his face was tired and dirty, but he lifted his hat politely and looked up at the woman.

Then his eyes opened wide in surprise. The woman stared down at him, equally surprised. Gabriel Oak and his cold-hearted love, Bathsheba Everdene, were face to face.

Bathsheba did not speak, and after a moment Gabriel said, in a quiet, sad voice, 'Do you want a shepherd, Miss?'

Bathsheba was not embarrassed, but she was certainly surprised. Life had clearly been unkind to Gabriel Oak, and she felt sorry for him.

'Yes,' she said slowly, 'I do want a shepherd, but . . .'

One of the villagers spoke up warmly for Gabriel. 'He's just the man you need, Miss. Look how he fought that fire!'

'Very well,' said Bathsheba. 'Then tell him to speak to my

farm manager.' She nodded to Gabriel in a businesslike way, and then rode off into the darkness.

The farmworkers began to return to the village. Gabriel talked to the farm manager about his new job, then he too followed the road to the village. As he walked, he thought with surprise about Bathsheba. How she had changed! She was no longer a shy young girl, but the proud and independent owner of a large farm.

Deep in his own thoughts, he did not at first notice a young girl waiting quietly on the road just outside the village. The girl seemed a little nervous, and Gabriel stopped and spoke kindly to her for a few moments. The girl replied shyly, in a soft, attractive voice, but when Gabriel gently advised her to go home, she said quickly, 'Oh no! Thank you, but I must wait . . . Please don't say anything about me in the village. I don't want people to know anything about me.'

Gabriel felt sorry for her, and although he had very little money himself, he gave her a few pence, which she took gratefully.

Gabriel spent the evening in the village pub with the other farmworkers. He listened with interest and amusement, mixed with a little sadness, to the talk about Miss Everdene, the farmer. He was too sensible to think that Bathsheba would ever marry him now, but his heart told him that she was still the woman he loved.

♦

The next morning, the first day of Gabriel's new job as a shepherd, there was great excitement in Weatherbury. Everybody was talking about two pieces of news. First, Miss Everdene had discovered that her farm manager was a thief. She had sent him away, and intended to manage the farm herself. The old men in the village shook their heads doubtfully over this. The second piece of news was the mysterious disappearance of Fanny Robin, Miss Everdene's youngest servant. She had not come home last night. The villagers searched everywhere for her, but she could not be found. Then in the evening came more news from Casterbridge. Fanny had run away with a soldier. Gabriel Oak remembered the nervous young girl he had met on the road outside the village. But it was too late to help her now, so he said nothing.

Chapter 3   A Joke for Valentine's Day

That same night, many miles north of Weatherbury, snow was falling on a path between a river and a high wall. The night was silent, then came a sudden small sound. A stone hit one of the windows in the high wall, then another stone, and another. The window opened, and a man's head appeared.

'Is that Sergeant Troy?' came a frightened voice from the snow.

The man stared down into the dark and the snow. 'Yes,' he said at last. 'What girl are you?'

'Oh, Frank, don't you know me?' said the voice sadly. 'It's Fanny Robin.'

'Fanny! What are you doing here?'

'But Frank, you said that I could come. And Frank, when will it be?'

'What?'

'Oh, Frank, don't speak like that! Our wedding – when shall we be married? You promised me so many times and I . . .' The sad little voice shook and could not continue.

'Don't cry! It's foolish. Of course we shall be married. I'll meet you in the town tomorrow morning, and we'll plan the wedding. I was surprised to see you here, that's all.'

'I'll go away now. Goodnight, Frank.'

'Yes, I'm sorry, Frank. I'll go away now. Goodnight, Frank.'

The window closed, and a small shadow moved away from the wall and disappeared into the snow.

◆

In Weatherbury, life continued as usual. On market days the talk was often about Farmer Bathsheba Everdene, who managed her own farm and did her own business in the market. The men farmers admired her soft dark eyes and beautiful young face, but they discovered that she argued over prices with them as strongly as any man.

Which attractive young woman does not like to receive admiration? Bathsheba was only human, and enjoyed very much the admiring looks that came from all the men. From all except one, that is.

That was Farmer Boldwood, a rich, good-looking man of about forty, who had a big farm at Weatherbury. He was unmarried, and seemed to be quite uninterested in the pretty face and fine eyes of Miss Everdene. Bathsheba began to wonder if he disliked all women, or if his heart had been broken in the past.

One Sunday she was talking with Liddy, the young girl who lived with her. Liddy had been born in Weatherbury and knew everything about the people there.

'Did you see Mr Boldwood in church this morning?' she asked Bathsheba. 'He was sitting opposite you, but he didn't look at you once!'

'Why should he?' asked Bathsheba, annoyed. 'I didn't ask him to.'

'Oh well, it's not surprising, I suppose,' said Liddy. 'He's a very proud man.'

Bathsheba pretended not to hear this. There was silence for a few minutes, then Liddy laughed.

'Tomorrow is the 14th February, St Valentine's Day,' she said. 'Why don't you send silly old Boldwood a valentine card? That would make him think!'

Bathsheba smiled. 'Actually, I've got a valentine card in my desk. I was going to send it to the neighbour's young son.' She gave a little laugh. 'Perhaps I should send it to Mr Boldwood instead!'

'Oh yes!' said Liddy, enthusiastically. 'It would be a great joke! And he'll never know who sent it, after all.'

And so, laughing and joking, the two young women got out the valentine card, and soon it was on its way to the post office. Inside the card, written in large letters, were the words 'M A R R Y M E'.

◆

What small things change people's lives! A stone thrown into a still pool of water is soon forgotten, but the effect on the water can go on for a long time. Little Fanny Robin knew this. In a cold northern town, she waited nervously in a church for Sergeant Troy, but Sergeant Troy never came. Perhaps she went to the wrong church, perhaps she went on the wrong day. Perhaps Sergeant Troy met her in another church, in another place. Perhaps.

Chapter 4   'I Want You as My Wife'

Farmer Boldwood was not used to jokes. He was a serious and lonely man, with no family or close friends. To him the valentine card seemed both mysterious and important. He thought about it all day and all night. Who had sent it? What kind of woman was she?

The next morning, the postman delivered a letter addressed to Gabriel Oak. When Boldwood realized the mistake, he decided to take the letter himself out to the fields, where Gabriel was working with the sheep.

There had been snow in the night, but the sun came up in a sky brilliant with red and orange, like the flames of a fire. Gabriel opened and read his letter, then showed it to Boldwood. The letter was from Fanny Robin, thanking Gabriel for his kindness and telling him that she would soon be the wife of Sergeant Troy.

'What kind of man is this Sergeant Troy?' asked Gabriel. He knew that Farmer Boldwood knew all the local people.

'Not the marrying kind, I'm afraid,' said Boldwood. 'Poor little Fanny!'

The two men shook their heads sadly, and Boldwood turned to go. Then he turned back. 'Oh, Oak,' he said carelessly, 'I wonder if you know this writing?' He pulled an envelope out of his pocket.

Gabriel looked at it, and said at once, 'Yes, it's Miss Everdene's.' His eyes went quickly to Boldwood's face, but, with a nod of thanks, Boldwood had gone.

♦

Farmer Boldwood had never thought much about women before; they were a mystery to him. Local people thought of him as a quiet, serious man, but behind that calm face there were deep, strong feelings. He could not stop thinking about Bathsheba now. On market days he stared at her all the time, noticing her black hair, the roundness of her chin, the softness of her cheeks. Slowly he realized that she was beautiful, and his heart began to move within him.

As winter turned into spring, people began to be busy in the fields once more. Boldwood was often near Bathsheba's fields, and it was not chance that took him there. Once, he saw her with Gabriel Oak and another farmworker, and he walked over to speak to her. But at the last minute he changed direction and walked away, his face red with shyness and uncertainty.

Bathsheba had soon realized that Boldwood knew who had sent the valentine card. His eyes now followed her everywhere and she had begun to feel a little uncomfortable, a little ashamed of her 'joke'. She did not want him to fall in love with her, and decided that in future she must behave very correctly towards him.

But the stone had been thrown into the pool, and already the circles of water were moving outwards quite quickly. At the end of May, Farmer Boldwood made his decision. Love for

But now Boldwood had begun to speak, he could not stop. He told her that he loved her wildly with all his heart.

Bathsheba now burned in him like a great fire, and he knew he must do something about it.

He found her down at the sheep-washing pool, watching her farmworkers as they pushed the sheep through the water. He asked her to walk with him by the river, and almost at once, he turned to her and said, very seriously, 'Miss Everdene! I feel – almost too much – to think. My life is not my own since I have seen you clearly. I have come to make you an offer of marriage. Beyond all things, I want you as my wife.'

Bathsheba was both embarrassed and afraid. What harm she had done with her silly valentine! 'Mr Boldwood,' she began, 'although I like and admire you, I cannot . . . it is not possible for me . . .' She could not go on.

But now Boldwood had begun, he could not stop. He told her that he loved her wildly with all his heart, that he would look after her all her life, that he would give her anything in the world she wanted.

As gently as she could, Bathsheba replied that she did not love him, and could not marry him.

'But you gave me hope, Miss Everdene.'

'Oh, please forgive me, sir! That valentine was so foolish – it was thoughtless of me. I am so sorry!' Bathsheba was frightened by the strong feelings shown in his face.

'Don't say that you can never love me,' he went on quickly. 'Let me speak to you again.'

'Mr Boldwood, I must think. Please give me time.'

'Yes, of course I will give you time,' he said gratefully. 'I am happier now – if I can hope.'

He left her then, and Bathsheba returned to the sheep-washing, worried and unhappy. She knew she did not love Boldwood, but she felt guilty about him. She did not know what to do.

A little later, she thought of another worry, and called Gabriel

Oak over to her. 'Gabriel, did any of the men see me with Mr Boldwood by the river?' she asked carefully.

'Yes, they did.'

'And did they say anything?'

'They said that you and Farmer Boldwood would be in church together before long.'

'Well, that's quite untrue! And I want you to tell everybody that.'

Gabriel gave a little smile. 'I see,' he said quietly. He had guessed about the valentine to Boldwood, and because of his own deep, silent love for Bathsheba, he could recognize another man in love.

'I don't suppose, Bathsheba,' he continued, 'that you want my opinion.'

'Miss Everdene, you mean,' Bathsheba said coldly. She felt confused. She knew Gabriel was an honest, intelligent man, and she valued his opinion greatly.

'Well, what is your opinion?' she said quietly.

'That you have not behaved like a thoughtful, kind and honest woman.'

In a second, Bathsheba's face was bright red. 'I'm not in the least interested in your opinion!' she said angrily. 'I suppose you think I should marry *you*!'

'No,' said Gabriel coolly, 'I neither think that nor wish it. But if you don't love a man, Miss Everdene, it's a cruel joke to send him a valentine.'

Bathsheba was now too angry to stop herself. 'You'll leave my farm at the end of this week,' she said wildly.

'Very well,' said Gabriel calmly. 'But I'd prefer to go at once.'

'Then go!'

Chapter 5   Bathsheba's Terms

Twenty-four hours later, sixty of Bathsheba's sheep broke out of their field and got into a field of young corn. Sheep are silly animals, and they ate and ate the new corn until their stomachs were twice the usual size. Green corn does terrible things inside the body, and so Jan Coggan and the other workers ran to find Bathsheba at the farmhouse.

'Oh, Miss Everdene, the sheep've been in the new corn,' called Jan Coggan.

'And they'll all be dead in an hour or two!' said Joseph Poorgrass.

Bathsheba ran with them back to the field. Most of the sheep were already lying helplessly on the ground.

'What can we do to save them?' cried Bathsheba. 'There must be something!'

'You have to push a pin in their sides to let out the gas and air,' Jan Coggan said. 'But it's hard to find the right place – you can kill the sheep easily.'

'There's only one man round here who can do it,' said Joseph Poorgrass. 'And that's Shepherd Oak. He's a clever man, he is.'

'I don't want to hear his name again!' Bathsheba said angrily. 'I will never send for him – never!'

Just then one of the sheep jumped in the air, fell heavily and lay still. Bathsheba went up to it. The sheep was dead.

'Oh, what shall I do?' she cried. 'I won't send for him!'

But she knew she had to. She turned quickly to Jan Coggan. 'Go and find Oak and tell him he must come at once.'

Twenty minutes later, Coggan was back with a long face. 'He won't come unless you ask him politely,' he said.

Another sheep fell down and died. 'How can he be so cruel?' Bathsheba's eyes filled with tears.

'He'll come if you ask him,' said Joseph Poorgrass. 'He's a good, true man, is Shepherd Oak.'

'He'll come if you ask him,' said Joseph Poorgrass. 'He's a good, true man, is Shepherd Oak.'

Quickly, Bathsheba went back to the house and wrote Gabriel a note. At the end she wrote, '*Please don't leave me, Gabriel.*'

Half an hour later, Gabriel was hard at work among the sheep. It was a difficult and unpleasant job, but he saved all the sheep except four. When he eventually finished, he was tired and dirty. Bathsheba came and looked him in the face.

'Gabriel, will you stay on with me?' She smiled hopefully.

Love is a golden prison. 'I will,' said Gabriel.

And Bathsheba smiled at him again.

♦

It was not a wise decision. Gabriel knew he should move on. He knew he could find better, more independent work and begin to make something more of his life. But he could not break away from Bathsheba, even though he believed that she would become the wife of Farmer Boldwood before the summer was over.

Soon came the time for sheep-shearing, when all the wool was cut off and the sheep looked like new animals in their smooth, pink skins. After the work was finished, there was always a big supper for the workers in the farmhouse. Farmer Boldwood came, and Gabriel saw sadly that he was a welcome guest to Bathsheba.

After the supper and the singing, the farmworkers went home, but there was still a light in the farmhouse. Boldwood and Miss Everdene were alone, and Boldwood waited with burning eyes for Bathsheba's answer.

'I will try to love you,' she said at last, in an uncertain voice, 'and if I can, I will become your wife. But, Mr Boldwood, I cannot promise tonight. You say you will be away from home for six weeks, and at the end of that time, I hope I shall be able to give you my promise.'

'It is enough, Miss Everdene. With those dear words, I can wait.' He took her hand for a minute, and then quickly left.

♦

As she was her own farm manager, it was always Bathsheba's practice to walk round her farm at night to make sure that everything was locked and safe. There was a cloudy sky that night, and the path back to the farmhouse went through a small, dark wood. As Bathsheba hurried through the trees, she heard somebody coming down the path towards her. They met at the darkest place in the wood and as they passed each other, Bathsheba felt something catch at her skirt and pin it to the ground.

'Sorry!' said a man's voice, in surprise. 'Have I hurt you?'

'No,' said Bathsheba. She pulled at her skirt, but could not get it free.

'Wait a minute,' said the man. He bent down to look. 'I see what's happened. My boot is caught in your skirt. If you stand still a minute, Miss, I'll get it free.'

At that moment, the moon broke through the clouds, and in its soft, ghostly light Bathsheba could see the stranger clearly. He was a soldier, a tall young man in a bright red coat with shiny buttons. He looked hard into her face, and smiled with admiration. Bathsheba immediately looked away.

'I can do it,' she said quickly, and pulled at her skirt. But the skirt was firmly held and would not come free.

The soldier bent down again, and although his fingers were busy, the job seemed to take him a very long time. He looked up into her face.

'My boot is caught in your skirt. If you stand still a minute, Miss,
I'll get it free.'

'You are a prisoner, Miss,' he said, amused. 'I must cut your skirt if you're in a hurry.'

'Yes, please do,' said Bathsheba, embarrassed and a little angry at the soldier's smile.

The young man smiled again. 'Thank you for showing me that beautiful face,' he said pleasantly.

'I didn't choose to do it,' Bathsheba said, her face red. 'Now please untie my skirt quickly, and go away!'

'That's not very kind,' said the soldier with a laugh. 'I've seen a lot of women in my life, but I've never seen a woman as beautiful as you. This happy accident will be over too soon for me!'

Bathsheba said nothing and tried not to look at him. At last, the skirt was free, and the soldier stood up. Bathsheba moved quickly away down the path.

'Ah, Beautiful, goodbye!' the soldier called after her.

Bathsheba hurried home, her eyes bright and her cheeks still pink with embarrassment.

It was a very great mistake of Boldwood's that he had never once told her she was beautiful.

Chapter 6 The Long Bright Sword

A week or two later, the hay-making began, and every man and woman who could walk was out in the fields, cutting the long sweet grass in the warm sunshine. When Bathsheba went down to watch, she saw a stranger helping with the hay wagons – a stranger in a bright red coat.

She had asked Liddy about him, and Liddy had told her that he was a clever young man, who could be more than just a soldier if he wanted. He had come back to stay in his village for a time, and his name was Sergeant Troy.

When he saw Bathsheba watching the hay-making, he walked over to talk to her. He asked politely, but with a laugh in his eyes, if he could help on her farm while he was staying in Weatherbury.

There was no doubt that Sergeant Troy was a clever, handsome young man, who knew exactly how to please a woman. He knew the right words to say, when to laugh and joke, and when to be serious. Bathsheba's feelings were very confused, she did not know if she was angry with him or pleased.

After that, Troy came often to the farm to help with this job or that. He was a man who lived for the moment. He never thought about yesterday, or tomorrow, and telling lies was for him as easy as breathing. So it was natural for him to tell Bathsheba that he loved her. And it was hard for Bathsheba not to believe him.

One day, Troy asked her if she had ever seen the famous sword-practice of the soldier. Bathsheba had not, and though she was a little afraid of the idea, she agreed she would like to see it.

They met on a hill near Weatherbury. It was a golden midsummer evening, and the sunlight danced among the green shadows of the grass and trees. It shone also on Sergeant Troy's long, bright sword.

'Now,' said the soldier. 'I shall show you the art of sword-fighting.' His sword cut quickly through the air, upwards, downwards, sideways.

'How bloodthirsty it looks!' said Bathsheba, fearfully.

Troy laughed. 'Now, I'll be more interesting and fight you – but not really, of course! You mustn't move or breathe. I won't touch you, but you must keep perfectly still.'

So Bathsheba stood very still, and in a frightening, wonderful dance, the shining sword moved like lightning all round her body – in and out like a snake's tongue, up, down, backwards, forwards. She was enclosed in a circle of bright light.

Then the sword was still. 'Your hair is untidy,' said Troy softly,

*The sword whispered past her ear, and a small piece of hair
fell to the ground.*

before she could move or speak. 'Wait. I'll do it for you.' The sword whispered past her ear, and a small piece of hair fell to the ground.

Bathsheba found her breath again. 'Oh, it's magic! I thought you'd killed me!'

'No, no,' smiled Troy. 'My sword never makes mistakes.' He picked up the piece of hair. 'I must leave you now. I'll keep this as my memory of today.'

He came closer to her. A minute later, he was gone, his red coat bright among the trees. But that minute had sent the blood up into Bathsheba's face, and a burning feeling all over her. Troy had bent his head and kissed her on the mouth.

♦

When a warm-hearted and independent woman like Bathsheba Everdene falls in love, her feelings are often stronger than her good sense. Bathsheba could see nothing wrong in her brave soldier. To her, Sergeant Troy was as good and true a man as the patient, hard-working Gabriel Oak.

Gabriel had watched Troy's obvious success with great sadness, and not a little worry. When he saw a chance, he planned to speak to Bathsheba, to try to warn her.

His chance came one evening, when he met Bathsheba out walking through the cornfields. He turned to walk with her.

'It's late for you to be out alone, Miss Everdene. But perhaps Mr Boldwood is coming to meet you?' Gabriel knew very well that Boldwood was away from home, but he had to begin the conversation somewhere.

Bathsheba's eyes were angry. 'Why do you speak of Mr Boldwood? It's quite true that he has asked me to marry him, but I am not going to. When he returns home, I shall tell him.'

There was a short silence. Then Gabriel tried again.

'Young Sergeant Troy is not good enough for you, Miss. He

might be a clever man and a brave soldier, but you mustn't believe everything he tells you.'

'Why not?' She did not wait for an answer. 'He's as good as any man in this village. I don't know why you speak of him like that.'

Gabriel was silent again. The name of Fanny Robin was in his mind, but he did not say it. He tried one last time.

'You know, Bathsheba, that I love you, and will always love you. Now I am poor, I know I can never marry you, but I want to see you safe and happy. Why don't you marry Mr Boldwood? He loves you, and you would be safe with him. Please, my dear, be careful of this soldier.'

Bathsheba turned her face away. Her hands were shaking a little, and she replied in a low voice, 'I won't let you talk to me like this. I want you to go away and leave the farm.'

'Don't be foolish,' said Gabriel gently. 'You've done that once, and you know you can't manage without me on this farm. I speak to you like this because I love you and care about you. You can't blame me for that!'

It is difficult to be angry with a man who tells you, calmly and firmly, that he loves you. Bathsheba said no more, only that she wanted to be alone. Gabriel stood and watched her walk away, and a few minutes later, he saw a red coat coming towards her on the path. Gabriel turned sadly back to the village.

Chapter 7   The Jealous Lover

Bathsheba found that she could not wait until Boldwood's return, so she sent him a letter. She wrote that she had thought carefully about his offer, but had decided she could not marry him.

Sergeant Troy had also gone away for a few days to visit

friends, and Bathsheba had time to think. But she could not think clearly about anything, and her moods changed from minute to minute. Liddy found her very difficult to live with.

'But, Miss,' she said, 'you said only this morning that Sergeant Troy was a very wild young man and . . .'

'Oh Liddy! How can you be so silly? Of course he's not wild! You don't really believe that he's bad, do you?'

'Yes. No. Oh, I don't know what to say,' said poor Liddy nervously. 'Do you love him, then, Miss?'

'Of course I love him!' cried Bathsheba angrily. 'Can't you see that? Oh Liddy,' she went on in a quieter voice, 'Love is a terrible thing – it brings nothing but worry, and pain, and unhappiness.'

♦

Farmer Boldwood knew that as well. Bathsheba's letter, and the rumours in Weatherbury about Troy, had killed his hope of happiness. He moved like a man in a black dream.

The day after his return, he met Bathsheba out walking near the village. Bathsheba tried not to stop, but Boldwood stood in her path, and talked wildly of his broken heart and her broken promises. He told her that she was cruel, heartless, that she had given him hope and then taken it away again.

It is a sad thing to see a strong man who cannot control his feelings. Bathsheba pitied him greatly and tried to answer him kindly, but when he began to talk about Sergeant Troy, she became frightened. His words were even wilder now, he called Troy a thief – a shameless, greedy man who stole other people's happiness with lies and kisses.

This violent jealousy frightened Bathsheba very much. She decided to go and find Troy, and to warn him to stay away from Weatherbury until Boldwood was calmer. She left home secretly that evening, and was away for a week. No one knew where she had gone, and there was much talk in the village. Gabriel Oak was silent and unsmiling, and feared the worst.

Bathsheba arrived home one evening a week later, looking tired and worried. Gabriel was very glad to see her home again, and tried to forget the rumours about her disappearance. Later, when he was walking home, he passed a man coming towards the farm. 'Goodnight, Gabriel,' the passer said.

It was Boldwood. 'Goodnight, sir,' Gabriel said. He went on to his house and went indoors to bed.

Farmer Boldwood walked on towards Bathsheba's house. The violent feelings of a week ago were cooler now. He wanted to apologize to Bathsheba and ask her to forgive him. But at the door Liddy told him, nervously, that Miss Everdene could not see him.

Boldwood turned away without a word. Clearly, she had not forgiven him. He did not hurry home, and as he walked through the village, he saw a wagon stopping at the village pub. A man in a red coat got out.

Boldwood stopped. 'Ah,' he said to himself, 'the successful lover.' The man came up the road and Boldwood stepped out in front of him.

'Sergeant Troy, I wish to speak a word with you,' he said. 'I am William Boldwood.'

Troy looked at him. It was past ten o'clock and the villagers were all in bed. Boldwood was a big man, and was carrying a heavy stick. It seemed wise to be polite.

'Yes,' Troy said quietly. 'What about?'

'I know quite a lot about Fanny Robin's love for you. I don't know where she is now, but you ought to find her, and marry her.'

'I suppose I ought to. But I can't. I'm too poor.' There was an unpleasant smile on Troy's face.

'I'll give you money,' said Boldwood quickly. 'Fifty pounds

Boldwood lifted his stick and Troy backed away from him.

now, and five hundred on your wedding day. But marry Fanny and go away from here. Leave Miss Everdene alone. She's too good for you.'

'Fifty pounds now, you said?' Troy looked thoughtful. 'Well, perhaps I do like Fanny best. But Bathsheba is waiting for me, you know. I am staying with her tonight.'

Boldwood stared at him wildly. 'Staying the night?' he whispered. 'My God, I'll kill you!' He lifted his stick and Troy backed away from him.

'I can't marry them both, can I?' he said, with a laugh. 'But perhaps I'll marry Fanny. I need the money.'

The laugh seemed to ring for ever in Boldwood's ears. 'You must marry Bathsheba at once,' he said violently. 'You can't leave her now, you black-hearted dog! I'll give you money.'

'You can keep your money, Boldwood,' Troy said unpleasantly. 'You can't buy *me*. And you're too late.' He pulled a piece of paper from his pocket and held it under Boldwood's nose. 'Take a look at that. You'll see that I married Bathsheba last week!'

Chapter 8   Covering the Corn

One night, at the end of August, when Bathsheba had not been a married woman for very long, a man stood in her farmyard, looking up at the moon and sky. A hot wind was blowing from the south, and among the hurrying clouds the moon shone with a strange, hard light.

Gabriel Oak looked round the farmyard with worried eyes. The harvest had finished and there were eight enormous, uncovered piles of corn in the yard – most of the farm's riches for the year. Oak was a farmer to his bones. He knew that a storm was coming, and that after the thunder there would be violent, heavy rain. 'If that corn gets wet, it'll be a disaster,' he said to himself. 'She'll lose an awful lot of money.'

But Sergeant Troy now managed the farm for his wife, and he had chosen this night for the harvest supper and dance. Earlier, Gabriel had sent a message to him, saying that the corn should be covered. But a message had come back: 'Mr Troy says it will not rain.'

Gabriel decided that the corn must be covered that night, but he knew he would have to do the work alone. At the harvest supper, Troy had given all the farmworkers some very strong drink, and now they lay asleep on the floor and the tables, too drunk to move or lift a finger.

Moving quickly and silently in the dark, Gabriel found the ladder and the tools for making straw-covers. He carried straw up the ladder, sat on the top of the corn-pile, and with his tools began to tie the straw firmly together.

The wind had died now, and the air was heavy and hot. Then Gabriel heard thunder in the distance, and very soon the storm was all around him. Brilliant silver-blue lightning burst through the dark clouds, followed by deafening crashes of thunder. There was no rain yet, but Gabriel knew he must work fast.

Suddenly, he thought he saw somebody moving in the yard.

'Who is there?' came Bathsheba's voice from the darkness.

'Gabriel. I'm up on the top, making a straw-cover.'

'Oh, Gabriel! I'm so worried about the corn. Can we save it? Is my husband with you?'

'No.'

'Do you know where he is?'

Gabriel was silent, and after a pause Bathsheba said, 'Don't tell me. I know it all. The men are all drunk and asleep – my husband among them. And he promised me that the corn . . .' There was an unhappy silence. 'But Gabriel, can I do anything to help?'

'You can carry the straw up to me, if you're not afraid to come up the ladder in the dark. That would be a great help.'

So Gabriel and Bathsheba worked on together through the night, while the storm crashed around their ears. Once, the lightning was so violent that Bathsheba nearly fell off the ladder. Gabriel caught her arm and held her, and they watched in fear as the lightning hit a tall tree and burned it black in a second.

'How terrible!' whispered Bathsheba.

The rain had still not come, and after a time the storm became a little quieter. Bathsheba had not spoken for a long time, then she suddenly said, 'Gabriel, I want to explain something.' He turned to look at her.

'I went away, not to marry Troy, but to tell him it was finished,' she said quickly. 'I care for your good opinion, and I

*Once, the lightning was so violent that Bathsheba nearly fell
off the ladder. Gabriel caught her arm.*

wanted you to know that. You looked so seriously at me when I returned.'

'I see,' said Gabriel quietly.

'And then, when I met him, he told me that he had seen a woman more beautiful than me and . . . I was mad with jealousy, and so I . . . I married him! And now, not another word about it. I'll bring up some more straw.'

She went down the ladder and the work continued. Soon Gabriel saw that she was tired, and very gently, he told her to go indoors and rest.

She looked up into his face. 'Oh Gabriel, thank you for all your hard work for me, a thousand times!'

She disappeared into the darkness and Gabriel worked on alone, thinking about her story. She had spoken more warmly to him tonight than she had ever done before.

At five o'clock the wind came back and brought the rain, which fell out of the sky like stones. Soon, Gabriel was wet to the skin, but he fought on to finish the work. At about seven o'clock he climbed thankfully down the ladder for the last time, and set off for home. Not many people were out and Gabriel was surprised to see Farmer Boldwood walking slowly along the road under an umbrella.

Gabriel stopped to speak to him, and told him about his night's work to cover Bathsheba's corn. 'Your corn is all covered, I suppose, sir.'

'No,' said Boldwood slowly. 'No, I forgot about it.'

Gabriel stared at him. 'You'll lose it all, then, after this rain.'

But Boldwood did not seem to care. Gabriel was saddened to see the change in him. Here was a man who was even unhappier than himself.

'Things have gone wrong for me lately, Oak,' said Boldwood quietly. 'You probably know all about it.'

'Well, life never gives us what we want,' Gabriel said. They walked on together in silence.

Chapter 9   The Death of Fanny Robin

The summer passed, and autumn brought new worries to Bathsheba. One Sunday evening in the farmhouse, there was a coolness in the air. There had been an argument about money. It was not the first, and Bathsheba knew it would not be the last. But with her sweetest smile, she asked Troy to spend less money, and to stay at home more.

'There was a time not long ago, dear Frank, when you only wanted to be with me.'

Troy looked impatient. 'Why shouldn't I go out and enjoy myself? I'm not your prisoner.'

'Oh Frank, is that how you think of our life together? Perhaps I made a mistake in marrying you, but why must you be so unkind?'

'You knew what married life would be like,' said Troy angrily. 'Don't start complaining now.'

'But you do still love me, don't you, Frank?' Bathsheba's eyes were full of tears.

Troy did not reply and went quickly out of the room, shutting the door violently behind him.

A few months ago, Bathsheba had been a proud and independent woman. Now, she knew all the misery of a love that was not returned.

Early the next morning, Troy went out and drove off in the wagon to Casterbridge. A little later, Bathsheba walked round to the farmyard and saw Boldwood and Gabriel Oak in the distance down the road. They were deep in conversation, and as she watched, they called Joseph Poorgrass over and spoke to him.

Joseph then came down the road towards her, clearly with a message for her.

'Well, what is it, Joseph?' said Bathsheba.

'It's little Fanny Robin, Mrs Troy. She's dead in Casterbridge workhouse.'

'Fanny!' said Bathsheba in surprise. 'Oh, poor girl! What happened to her? What did she die of?'

'They didn't tell me that. But she's coming back here this afternoon, in Mr Boldwood's wagon. She belongs by law to this village, you see, and she'll be buried here tomorrow at the church.'

'Tell them to bring the coffin to my house for the night,' said Bathsheba quietly. 'She was my servant, although only for a short time. Poor, poor Fanny!'

She wondered why Gabriel had not brought the news himself. She remembered that Fanny had run away with a soldier back in February. Clearly, the soldier had not married her – and now she was dead in the workhouse. A small, worrying idea began to grow in her mind.

Later, she looked for Gabriel, but could not find him. In the village, there were little groups of people whispering together, but when she went past, they became silent and serious. Nobody seemed to want to talk to her. Her farmworkers would not look her in the face, and moved away quickly when she spoke to them. She went back to the house and found Liddy.

'There's something strange going on, about Fanny Robin. What is it?'

'Oh, just rumours from Casterbridge,' said Liddy quickly. 'Nothing, really.'

'What rumours? Tell me, Liddy. You must tell me!' Bathsheba said angrily. 'Why will nobody talk to me, or look at me?'

'It's just a silly story,' Liddy said nervously, 'that . . . that Mr Troy was Fanny's soldier sweetheart. Nobody believes it really.'

Bathsheba's face was white. 'Oh, they do believe it, Liddy, they do! And what did Fanny die of, Liddy?' she whispered. 'What stories do they tell about that?'

But Liddy did not know, or would not say.

That evening, Fanny Robin's plain, wooden coffin lay in the front room of the farmhouse. The house was still and quiet, but Bathsheba could not sleep. Troy had not yet come home, and the terrible doubts in Bathsheba's mind were driving her mad. She held her head in her hot hands, and her confused thoughts ran round and round like frightened sheep. The story was true, she knew it was true. She remembered Gabriel's warnings to her last summer, she saw again the embarrassment and pity on all the faces around her today. And the cause of Fanny's death – why would no one tell her? She could guess the cause, oh yes, but she had to know . . . yes, she must know.

She picked up a light and went like a ghost into the front room. With shaking hands she took off the top of the coffin, and looked down on the still, white face of Fanny Robin – and her dead child. A long, low cry of pain whispered round the room. Bathsheba fell on her knees beside the coffin and covered her face with her hands, the hot tears running through her fingers.

Minutes or perhaps hours passed, and then Bathsheba heard the front door open and close. A second later, her husband was in the room.

'What's the matter, in God's name? Who's dead?' said Troy.

Bathsheba stared at him with wild eyes. Troy stepped up to the coffin and looked down. His face went as still as stone.

'Do you know her?' Bathsheba's voice seemed to come from a long way away.

'I do,' said Troy.

'And . . . and the child?' whispered Bathsheba.

Troy stepped up to the coffin and looked down. His face went as still as stone.

For the first time in his life Troy felt the full pain of shame and guilt. He bent slowly over the coffin, and gently kissed that still, white face.

'Don't – don't kiss them! Oh, Frank, kiss me too – kiss me!'

Troy turned to look at his wife. His eyes were stony. 'Why did you come into my life, with your handsome face and your womanly tricks!' He turned back to the coffin. 'Oh, Fanny, dear Fanny, I have been a bad, black-hearted man. But in the eyes of God, you are my real wife!'

A cry of pain burst from Bathsheba. 'If she's . . . that, . . . what . . . am I?'

'You are nothing to me – nothing,' said Troy heartlessly. 'This dead woman is more to me, than you ever were, or are, or can be.'

Without a word, Bathsheba turned and ran from the room, out of the house into the night.

◆

Troy spent the rest of that night with some painful thoughts. Until now, luck, a handsome face, and a quick mind had given him an easy life. Now, for the first time, he did not like himself. Fanny's dead face had filled him with guilt and shame, and a feeling of great sadness.

The next morning, he went into Casterbridge. He returned in the afternoon to the village church, and found the place where they had buried Fanny. On his knees in the rain, he planted spring, summer and autumn flowers in Fanny's memory. Then he turned his face away from Weatherbury, and set off on foot to find a new life.

Chapter 10   Boldwood Still Has Hope

About ten days later, news was brought to Bathsheba that her husband was dead. Somebody had found his clothes on the shore, and another person had seen him swimming out to sea. It was a dangerous place for swimming and everybody said that Troy must be dead. But his body was never found.

When Troy had left home, Bathsheba's feelings had been frozen – she had felt neither glad nor sorry. She knew that she belonged to him and that, sooner or later, he would be home again. Even when his clothes were brought home, she did not really believe that he was dead.

Kind little Liddy had looked after Bathsheba in the dark days after Fanny's burial. When the news about Troy came, she said carefully, 'We must buy you some black clothes to wear now.'

'No, no,' said Bathsheba hurriedly. 'He's still alive. I know.'

'How do you know that?' asked Liddy in surprise.

'If he was dead, I would know it – here.' She put her hand on her heart.

◆

The smell of autumn was now in the air, and the leaves began to turn brown and gold. Work on the farm had to go on, but Bathsheba had little enthusiasm for it. She did one sensible thing – she made Gabriel Oak her farm manager. In fact, he had done the work of a farm manager for months. The only difference was that he now earned more money.

On the neighbouring farm, Boldwood continued to live a sad and lonely life. Because of the rain, most of his corn had gone bad, and was given to the pigs to eat. He seemed to have little interest in the management of his farm, and he too made Gabriel his farm manager. Gabriel now had his own horse, and was busy from sunrise to sunset with the work of both farms, while the two owners sat sadly in their homes.

As the winter months passed, a small flame of hope began to burn in Boldwood's heart. His love for Bathsheba had never died, but had grown into a kind of secret madness. It was a passion he could not control, though he tried to hide it from the eyes of the world. Bathsheba had lost none of her beauty, but she was a quieter, gentler woman now, and to Boldwood she was even more attractive. He thought that perhaps she would have kinder feelings towards him, now that she knew how painful love could be. He waited hopefully for an opportunity to speak to her.

He had to wait until the following September. He met Bathsheba at the big sheep market near Casterbridge, and at the end of the day he offered to drive her home. It was already dark and Oak was too busy with the sheep to go with her. Bathsheba found it impossible to refuse.

For a time, Boldwood drove in silence, turning words over in his mind.

'I hope the sheep have sold well today, Mrs Troy,' he said at last, nervously.

'Oh yes, thank you,' said Bathsheba quickly.

They talked about the market and farming for some minutes, then Boldwood said suddenly and simply 'Mrs Troy, will you marry again some day?'

Bathsheba turned her head away in confusion. 'I have not thought of . . . of . . .'

'But your husband has been dead for nearly a year now.'

'His body was never found, so his death cannot be certain. And even if he is dead, I could not think of marrying.'

There was another silence.

'In law you can marry again after seven years – six years from now – whether his death is certain or not. And Bathsheba, oh my dear Bathsheba, at one time you were nearly mine, before you . . . But let's not talk of blame. I have never stopped loving you, never – not for one minute.' His voice shook with passion.

Bathsheba remembered how thoughtless, how unkind she had been to this man in the past, but he still loved her! Pity made her voice gentle.

'Six years is a long time.'

'But if I wait that time, will you marry me? If you pity me at all . . . If you are sorry for what you did . . . Oh Bathsheba, promise – promise me that in six years' time you will be my wife!'

His voice was so excited now that Bathsheba began to feel afraid. She knew she must choose her words carefully; she did not want to hurt this man again, but the violence of his feelings frightened her.

'What shall I do? You know that I cannot love you as a wife should. But if a promise to marry in six years' time can make you happy, then I . . . I will . . .'

'Promise!'

'Not now, no. But soon. At Christmas, I will tell you.'

'Christmas!' Boldwood was silent, then added, 'Well, I'll say no more until then.'

♦

Bathsheba's feelings were very confused. She did not know if she ought to give this strange promise or not. As Christmas came closer, she worried more and more. One day, when she was talking to Gabriel about farm business, she suddenly found that she was telling him all her troubles.

He listened carefully and seriously to her, and then said, 'It's certainly an unusual kind of promise. But since Boldwood's so unhappy, perhaps you should make this agreement with him. But is it right to think of marrying a man you don't love truly and honestly?'

'Perhaps it isn't, Gabriel. But I blame myself very much for his unhappiness. He never thought about me at all before I played that cruel trick on him. It will be a kind of punishment for me. But am I free to think of the idea of marrying again?'

'If you believe, as other people do, that your husband is dead, then yes.'

Bathsheba found this conversation unsatisfying. She had asked for his advice, and he had given it, coolly and sensibly. He had said not one word about his own love for her, or that he could wait for her as well as Boldwood. She did not *want* him to say that, of course, but . . . why hadn't he said it? It annoyed her all the afternoon.

Chapter 11   The Sergeant's Return

On Christmas Eve, there was much talk in the village about the big party that Farmer Boldwood was giving in the evening. Many people had been invited, and great preparations had gone on all day. Clearly, Boldwood intended to give everybody a truly wonderful time.

♦

In her room, Bathsheba was dressing for the party. She was not looking forward to it, because she knew she would have to give Boldwood an answer.

'How do I look, Liddy?' she said, as she looked in her mirror.

In her room, Bathsheba was dressing for the party. She was not looking forward to it.

'Oh, you look lovely,' said Liddy enthusiastically, 'so lovely that Mr Boldwood will want to run away with you!'

'Liddy, I don't want to hear any jokes like that,' said Bathsheba quietly. 'I don't want to go to this party, but I must. Now, get my coat, please. It's time to go.'

♦

Boldwood had finished dressing. He was both excited and nervous, and moved restlessly round the room. Gabriel Oak had come in to report on the day's work, and watched him sadly.

'You'll come tonight, Oak, won't you? I want you to enjoy yourself. I have great hopes that my future will be brighter soon. I am certain, yes, certain of her promise tonight, Oak.'

'Six years is a long time, sir,' said Gabriel quietly. 'A lot can happen in that time. It's best not to be too hopeful.'

'No, no,' said Boldwood impatiently. 'If she gives me her promise, she'll keep it – I know she will!'

♦

In a pub in Casterbridge another guest was preparing for the party – an uninvited guest.

Troy was not in a good mood. Luck had saved his life at sea a year ago – a passing boat had picked him up – but since then, luck had been absent from his life. He disliked hard work, but he liked the good things of life, and he could not get enough of them. For a long time, he had not wanted to return to Bathsheba, knowing that the ghost of Fanny would always come between them. But he had not a penny in his pocket, and Bathsheba's money and house and farm could give him an easy, comfortable life. He decided to go home.

In Casterbridge, he had heard the reports of his own death, and also rumours about his wife and Farmer Boldwood. These made him angry, and he decided to invite himself to Boldwood's Christmas party. He smiled when he thought of the effect that his arrival would have.

♦

Light shone out from all the windows in Boldwood's house. Guests moved from room to room and the small group of men outside in the dark could hear the sounds of laughing and talking and singing. The men whispered to each other in the shadows.

'I've heard he was seen in Casterbridge this afternoon.'

'Well, I believe it. His body was never found, you know.'

'It's a strange story. What will happen, do you think?'

'God knows. Poor young thing! But she was a fool to marry a man like that.'

Another man came down the path and joined the group. The whispers became more worried.

'He's here, in Weatherbury! I've seen him, with my own eyes!'

'Someone must go in and tell her. And Farmer Boldwood, too.'

'Not me! You go, Joseph Poorgrass. You're the oldest.'

'Let's wait a little. Perhaps he won't come here. Let's see what happens.'

♦

Inside the house, in a small back room, Boldwood held Bathsheba's hands in his own. His voice was low, passionate.

'Oh my love, my love! Say the words, give me your promise.'

Bathsheba felt too tired, too weak to fight him any longer. Tears ran down her face, as she whispered slowly, 'Very well. If my husband does not return, I'll marry you in six years from this day, if we both live.'

'Oh my dear, dear Bathsheba, thank you! I am happy now.'

He left the room, and some minutes later, when she was calmer, Bathsheba followed. She had put on her hat and coat, ready to leave, and on her way to the front door, she paused for a moment for a last look at the party. There was no music or dancing at that moment, and Boldwood was standing by the fireplace, alone. A group of villagers were whispering together in a corner.

Just then there was a loud knock on the door. A servant opened it, and said to Boldwood, 'It's a stranger, sir.'

Boldwood woke from his happy dream. 'Ask him to come in, and have a Christmas drink with us.' He looked round the room. 'And why is everybody so silent? Let's begin another dance.'

The servant at the door stepped back, and the stranger, his face hidden by the collar of his heavy coat, came into the room. Then he turned down the collar, and there was a sudden, deathly silence. Nobody moved or spoke. Troy began to laugh – a horrible sound in that still room.

He turned to Bathsheba. The poor girl's misery was by now beyond description. Her face was white, her mouth blue and dry, and her dark eyes stared into a distant hell.

Then Troy spoke. 'Bathsheba, I have come here for you!'

There was no movement, no reply.

Troy went across to her. 'Come, wife, do you hear what I say?' He spoke more loudly, but Bathsheba did not move.

A strange, thin, dry whisper came from Boldwood at the fireplace.

'Bathsheba, go with your husband!'

But Bathsheba's mind had stopped working. Impatiently, Troy reached out and caught her arm, but at his touch, she pulled away and gave a quick, low scream.

A moment later, there was a sudden deafening noise, and the room was filled with grey smoke. When the smoke cleared a little, the shocked guests saw Troy's body lying on the floor, his eyes already fixed in death. Then they looked at Boldwood, and saw in his hands one of the guns from the wall above the

*When the smoke cleared a little, the shocked guests saw Troy's body
lying on the floor, his eyes already fixed in death.*

fireplace. There was a mad light in Boldwood's eyes, and already he was turning the gun upon himself. One of his servants jumped up and knocked the gun out of his hands just in time. The bullet crashed into the ceiling.

'Well, it doesn't matter!' whispered Boldwood. 'There is another way for me to die.'

Quickly, he crossed the room to Bathsheba, and kissed her hand. Then he put on his hat, opened the door, and went out into the darkness.

Chapter 12   Arm-in-Arm

It was a long time before Weatherbury forgot the night of Mr Boldwood's Christmas party. The story was told, again and again, by fireplaces and in kitchens, at hay-making, and sheep-shearing, and harvest time. People remembered how Gabriel Oak had arrived five minutes after the shooting, and how Bathsheba had sent him for the doctor, although Troy was already dead. Bathsheba had taken his body home, and had washed and prepared it for burial with her own hands. People shook their heads over poor, mad Mr Boldwood. They remembered how he had walked through the night to Casterbridge and had knocked on the door of the prison. Then the door had closed behind him, and Mr Boldwood walked the world no more.

The punishment for murder was death, but Weatherbury did not think it was right for Boldwood to die. It had become clear that Boldwood's passion had sent him over the edge into madness. Letters about him were sent to London, and Weatherbury was very pleased when at last Gabriel Oak rode in from Casterbridge with the news: 'He's not going to die. It's prison for life, but not death.'

♦

By the summer, Bathsheba had begun to return to life. For months she had stayed in the house, seeing no one and talking to no one, not even Liddy. But now she spent more time in the open air and took a little interest in the farm again. One August evening, she walked into the village for the first time since that terrible Christmas night. She made a sad picture in the bright evening sunshine – with her long black dress, and her white, unhappy face.

As she passed the village church, she could hear singing inside and she stopped to listen. Perhaps it was the words that woke sleeping memories in her. But tears filled her eyes and she covered her face with her hands. When she lifted her head again, she saw Gabriel Oak standing a few yards away, watching her.

'Mr Oak,' she said, embarrassed, 'how long have you been here?'

'Only a few minutes, Mrs Troy,' Gabriel said politely.

Bathsheba dried her eyes with her handkerchief.

'Mrs Troy,' Gabriel said quietly, 'could I speak to you for a moment, about some business?'

'Oh yes, certainly.'

'The fact is, Mrs Troy, I probably won't be able to manage your farm for you much longer. I'm thinking of leaving England next spring, and going to America.'

Bathsheba stared at him in surprise. 'Leaving England! But everybody says that you're going to take poor Mr Boldwood's farm, and I thought you would still help me a little. Oh, Gabriel, what shall I do without you?'

Gabriel looked uncomfortable. 'Yes, I'm sorry, very sorry, but I . . . I think it's best to go. Good afternoon, Mrs Troy,' he finished quickly, and at once turned and walked away.

Bathsheba went home, her mind filled with a new trouble. This was actually quite good for her, because it pulled her out of her deep misery and made her think. She began to notice things that she had not seen before. She realized that Gabriel only came to the house when she was out, that he left messages for her in the farm office but did not wait to see her himself. Poor Bathsheba began to recognize a new misery in her life – her one true friend had grown tired of her at last. Through good times and bad times, he had been true and faithful to her, but now that she needed him more than ever, he was leaving her.

She lived through the autumn with these sad thoughts, and when Christmas came, it was not the memory of Boldwood's party that made her unhappy. As she came out of church, she looked round for Gabriel, and saw him hurrying away. The next day his letter arrived, saying that he would leave her farm at the end of March.

Bathsheba had never felt so miserable, so helpless. Her loneliness was so great that just after sunset she put on her coat and went down to Gabriel's house. She knocked quietly. Gabriel opened the door, and the moonlight shone on his kind, sensible face.

'Mr Oak,' said Bathsheba nervously.

Gabriel stared. 'Mrs Troy! What . . . But please come in.' He put a chair for her by the fire. 'I'm sorry it's not more comfortable, but I'm not used to lady visitors.'

'You'll think it strange that I have come, but . . . but I have been unhappy. I'm afraid that . . . that I have made you angry in some way.'

'Angry? No, you could never do that, Bathsheba!'

'Oh, I'm so glad!' she said quickly. 'But then why are you going away?'

'I've decided not to leave England, you know,' Gabriel

50

said quietly. 'I'm going to take Boldwood's farm, but I can't continue to work for you. Things have been said about us, you see.'

'What things?' said Bathsheba in surprise. 'What is said about you and me?'

'I cannot tell you.'

'But why not? You have always been honest with me in the past.'

'Well then, people say that I'm waiting around here with a hope of marrying you some day. You asked me to tell you, so you mustn't blame me.'

'Marrying me!' said Bathsheba quietly. 'I – yes, that idea is too silly – too soon, much too soon!'

'Yes, of course it's too silly, as you say.'

'Too . . . s-s-soon were the words I used.'

'I'm sorry, but you said "too silly".'

'I'm sorry too,' she replied, with tears in her eyes. 'I said "too soon", and I meant "too soon", Mr Oak. But it doesn't matter – not at all.'

Gabriel looked closely into her face, but the firelight was not bright enough for him to see much. 'Bathsheba,' he said at last, very gently, 'If I knew one thing – whether you would let me love you and win you, and marry you – if I only knew that!'

'But you never will know,' she whispered.

'Why?'

'Because you never ask.'

'Oh!' said Gabriel, with a quiet, delighted laugh. 'My dear love . . .'

'Why did you send me that unkind letter this morning? It was cruel!' There was a pinkness in Bathsheba's cheeks and a little of the old brightness in her eyes. 'I was the first sweetheart that you ever had, and you were the first I ever had.'

*'If I knew one thing,' he said, '– whether you would let me love
you and win you, and marry you . . .'*

'Oh, Bathsheba!' said Gabriel, laughing. 'You know very well
that I have always loved you. I've danced at your feet for many a
long mile, and many a long day!'

◆

And so a few weeks later, the two friends were quietly married,
and walked home from church arm-in-arm for the first time in
their lives.

The secret was soon known, and Weatherbury found the news
very pleasing. In the crowded village pub that evening, Jan
Coggan lifted his glass. 'Here's long life and happiness to
neighbour Oak and his lovely wife!' And there were nods
and smiles of agreement on every face.

ACTIVITIES

Chapters 1–3

Before you read

Note: The word *madding* means 'behaving madly'. It is uncommon and you may not find it in your dictionary.

1 This story is about farming in the nineteenth century. In what ways was farming then different from how it is today?

2 All these words come in this part of the story. Use a dictionary to check their meaning.

   corn farmyard lamb shepherd
   straw St Valentine's Day wagon

   Match each word to one of the meanings below:

   a a young sheep
   b a farm vehicle pulled by a horse
   c the seeds from which bread is made
   d the day when lovers send messages of love
   e the area and buildings round a farmhouse
   f used for beds for animals
   g a person who looks after sheep

After you read

3 These words describe some of the people in the story. Can you name them?

   a well-built/hard-working/calm/sensible
   b handsome/bright eyes/dark hair/attractive
   c young/nervous/soft voice/polite

4 Answer these questions:

   a Why does Gabriel Oak put on his best clothes to visit Bathsheba?
   b How does Gabriel lose all his money and his farm?
   c How do Gabriel and Bathsheba meet in Weatherbury and what does Gabriel ask for?

5 Answer these questions:

   a What is Fanny's job?   **b** Why does she run away?

6 Answer these questions:

  a What joke does Bathsheba play for St Valentine's Day?

  b What unexpected result does the joke have?

Chapters 4–5

Before you read

7 Would you like to work as a farmer and live in the countryside? Discuss your opinions with other students.

8 Sheep-*shearing* is part of the sheep farmer's year. *Shearing* means:

  a marking the sheep

  b cutting off the sheep's wool

  c collecting and then selling their wool

After you read

9 Who says these words? Who to?

  a 'I wonder if you know this writing?'

  b 'I suppose you think I should marry *you*!'

  c 'He won't come unless you ask him politely.'

  d 'Thank you for showing me that beautiful face.'

10 Answer these questions:

  a What arrangement does Bathsheba make with Boldwood at the sheep-shearing supper?

  b What accident brings Bathsheba and the soldier together? Can you guess the soldier's name?

Chapters 6–8

Before you read

11 These words come in the story. Use a dictionary to check their meaning:

  harvest hay-making sergeant sword

  Choose the right meaning for each word:

  a cutting and drying grass for winter food for animals

  b cutting, collecting and storing corn

    c like a knife but very long; used in the past by soldiers

    d a low-level officer in the army

12 Bathsheba now has three admirers. Can you guess which one she will choose? In her position, which one would *you* choose, and why? Discuss these questions with other students.

After you read

13 Answer these questions:

    a What moves 'in and out like a snake's tongue, up, down, backwards, forwards'?

    b Why does Troy perform for Bathsheba in this way?

    c Which of his actions show his daring behaviour towards Bathsheba?

14 Complete these sentences:

    a Boldwood moves like a man in a black dream because . . .

    b Boldwood offers Troy money because . . .

    c On the night of the harvest supper, Gabriel is worried because . . .

    d Bathsheba marries Troy because . . .

15 'Love is a terrible thing – it brings nothing but worry, pain and unhappiness.' Do you agree with Bathsheba or not? Discuss your views with other students.

Chapters 9–10

Before you read

16 These words come in the story. Use your dictionary to check their meaning.

bury coffin misery passion workhouse

Now match each word with the right meaning:

    a very strong feelings, such as anger or love

    b extreme unhappiness

    c to put a dead person in the earth

    d a place where very poor people were sent

    e the box in which a dead body is placed

17 Do you think this story will end well or badly? Why do you think so?

After you read

18 Answer these questions:
  a Whose coffin is brought to Bathsheba's front room?
  b What causes her death?
  c What effect does the dead person have on Troy?
19 'The two owners sat sadly in their homes.' Who are the two owners and why are they sad?

Chapters 11–12

Before you read

20 On page 50, we read that Gabriel had been *faithful* to Bathsheba. *Faithful* means:
  a loyal
  b honest
  c admiring

After you read

21 Answer these questions:
  a Why is Bathsheba not looking forward to the Christmas party?
  b Who is the 'uninvited guest'?
  c What happens to him?
22 Answer these questions:
  a Gabriel writes Bathsheba a letter. What message does it contain?
  b Later, he changes his plan of employment. In what way?
23 'That idea is too silly – too soon,' says Bathsheba. Why is her choice of words important and what does she mean?

Writing

24 'Love is a thief.' 'Love is a golden prison.' 'Love is a terrible thing.' What does Thomas Hardy mean by these three things?
25 You do not think that it is right that Boldwood should die because

he killed Troy. Write to the judge to tell him what you think. Begin like this:

Dear Sir,
I don't think it is right that William Boldwood should die. There are several reasons . . .

26 How does Bathsheba's character change during the story? What do you think makes her change?
27 Look at the picture on the front cover of this book. It shows a field at harvest time. After the harvest is completed, people usually have a service in church and a big party. What do people in *your* country do to celebrate the end of the harvest?
28 Have you ever seen a building on fire? Describe how the fire started and whether it was possible to put it out before the building was destroyed.
29 Write a note to a friend about this book. Say what things you liked about it and whether or not your friend will like it.

Answers for the Activities in this book are available from your local office or alternatively write to: Penguin Readers Marketing Department, Pearson Education, Edinburgh Gate, Harlow, Essex CM20 2JE.